EASY PIANO

A CHARLIE BROWN CHRISTMAS™

ISBN 978-0-634-02980-6

HAL•LEONARD® CORPORATION

7777 W. BLUEMOUND RD. P.O. BOX 13819 MILWAUKEE, WI 53213

PEANUTS © United Feature Syndicate, Inc.
www.snoopy.com

Visit Hal Leonard Online at
www.halleonard.com

PEANUTS © United Feature Syndicate, Inc.

CONTENTS

PEANUTS © United Feature Syndicate, Inc.

PEANUTS © United Feature Syndicate, Inc.

PEANUTS © United Feature Syndicate, Inc.

O TANNENBAUM

Traditional
Arranged by VINCE GUARALDI

Moderately slow

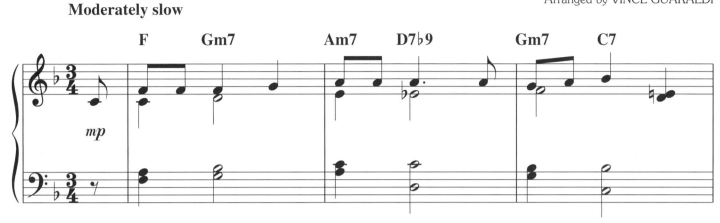

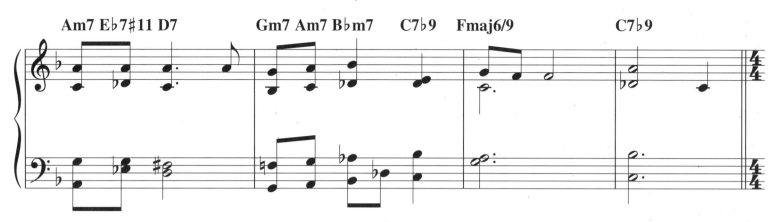

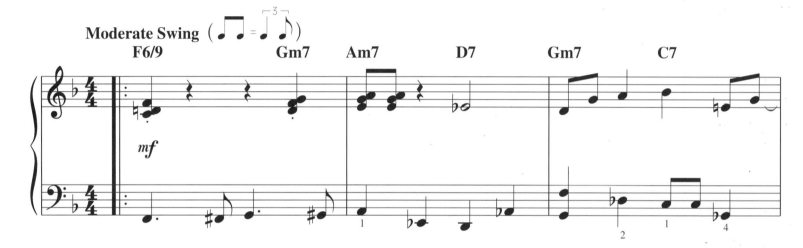

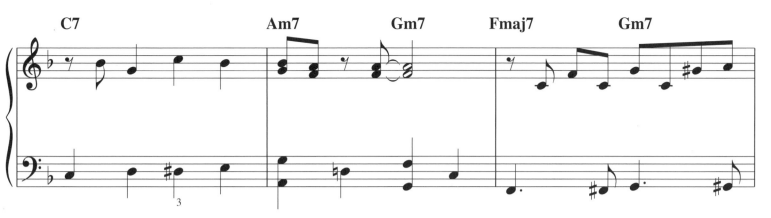

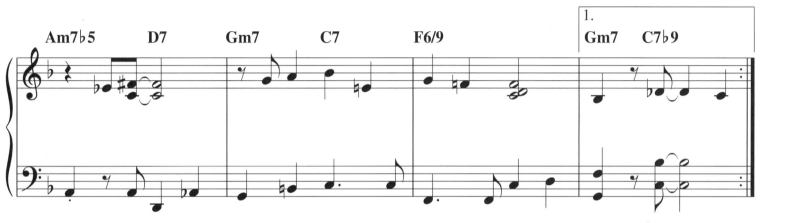

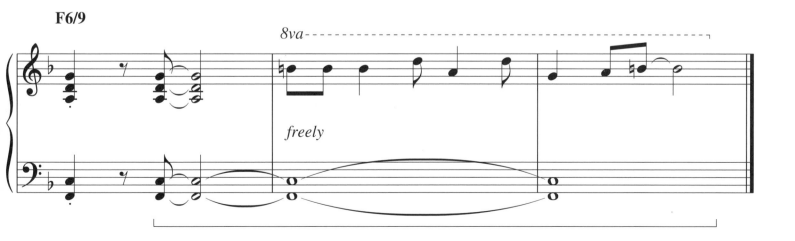

WHAT CHILD IS THIS

Traditional
Arranged by VINCE GUARALDI

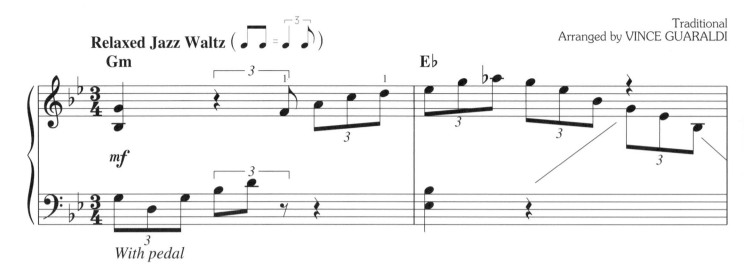

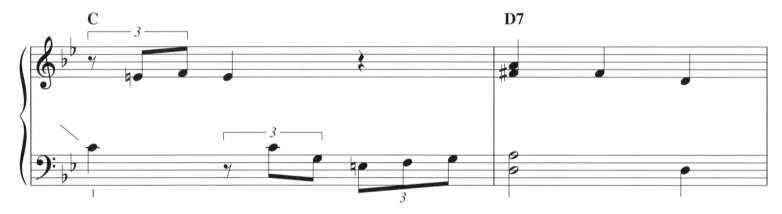

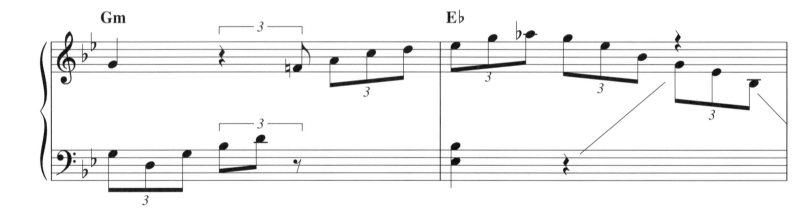

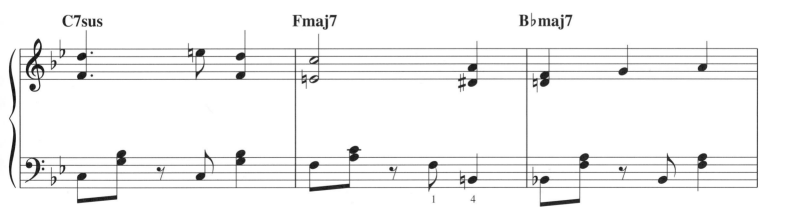

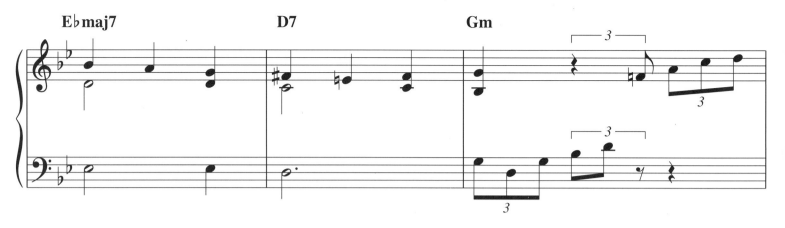

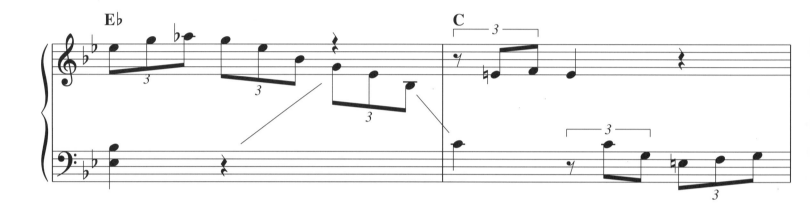

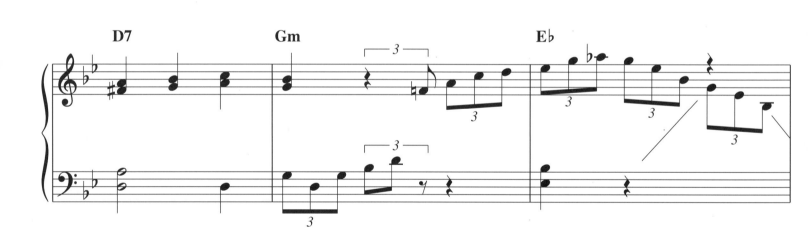

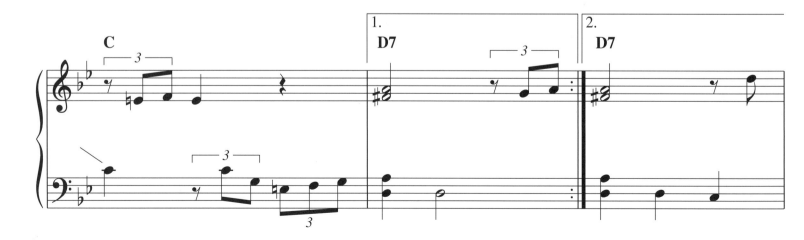

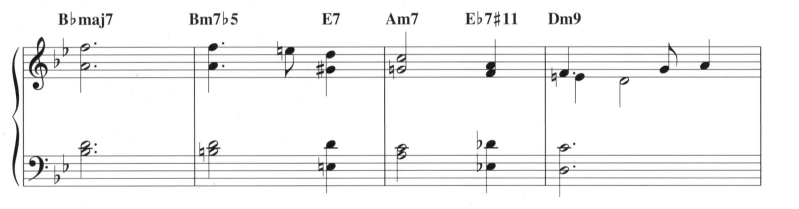

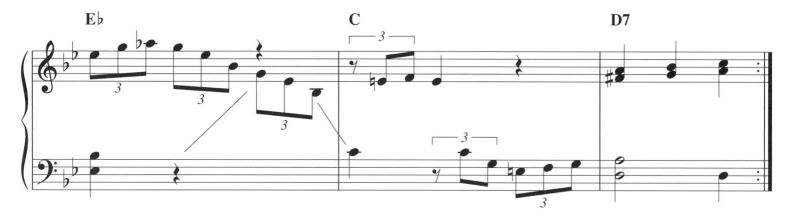

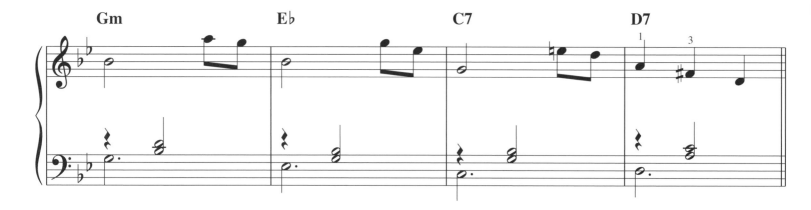

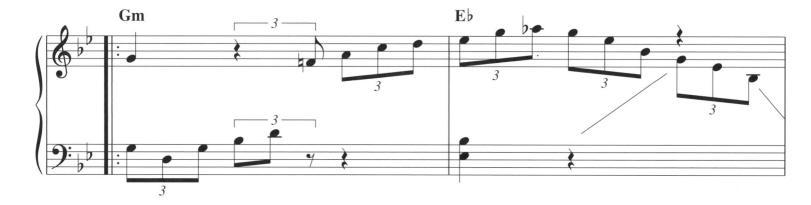

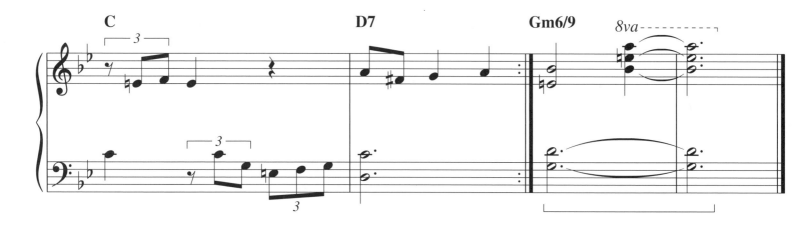

MY LITTLE DRUM

By VINCE GUARALDI

Moderately fast

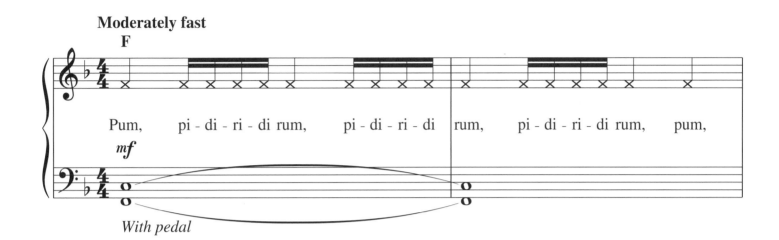

Pum, pi - di - ri - di rum, pi - di - ri - di rum, pi - di - ri - di rum, pum,

mf

With pedal

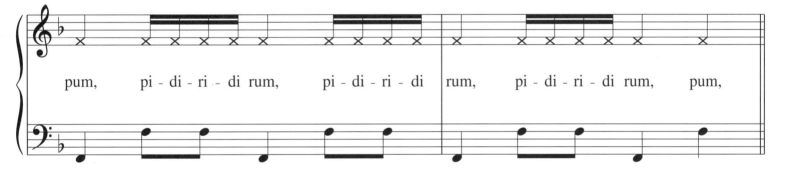

pum, pi - di - ri - di rum, pi - di - ri - di rum, pi - di - ri - di rum, pum,

(Background vocal continues)

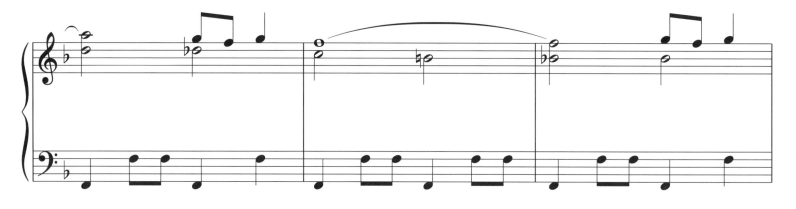

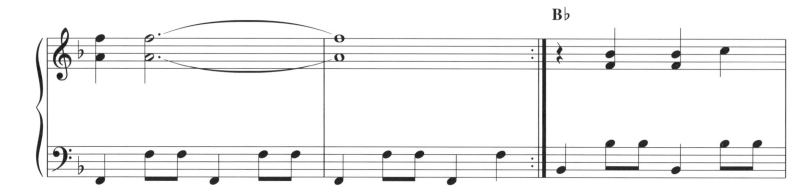

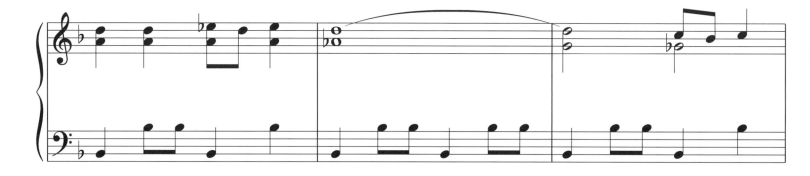

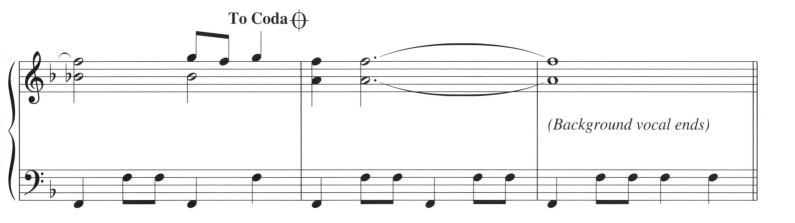

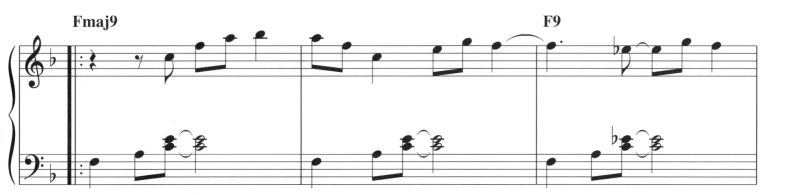

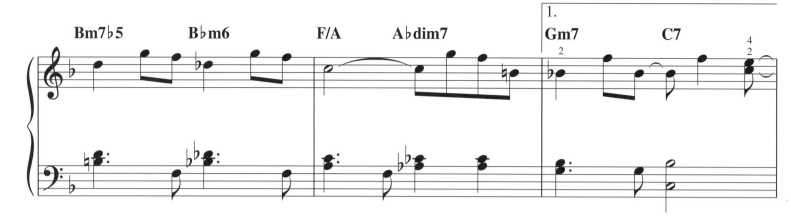

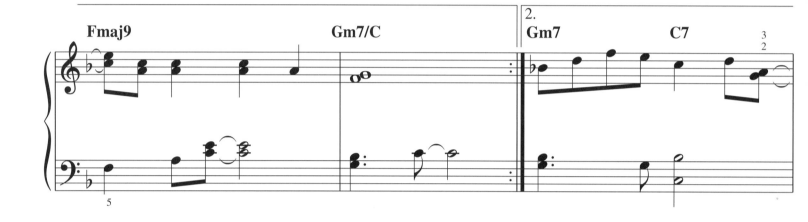

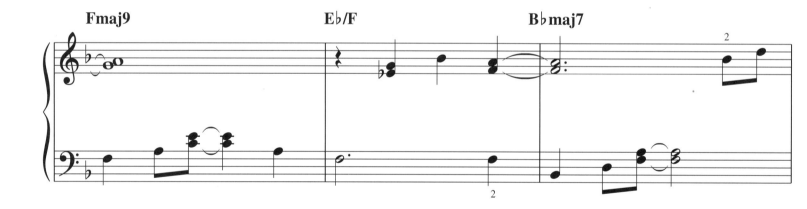

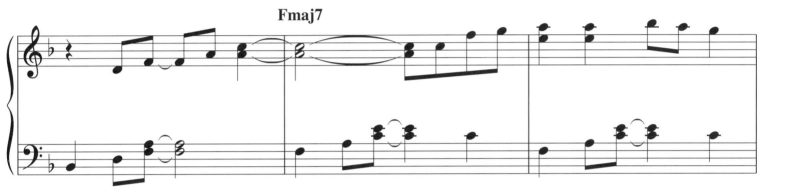

D.S. al Coda
(with repeat)

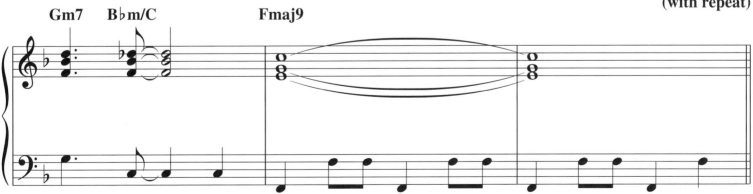

CODA

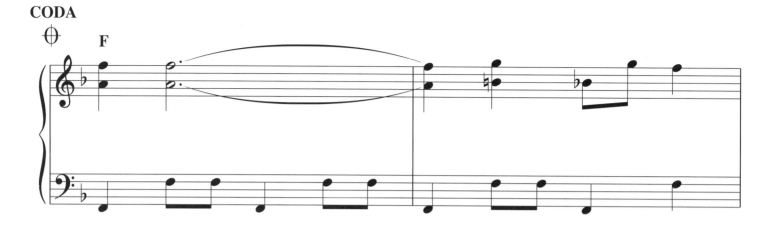

LINUS AND LUCY

By VINCE GUARALDI

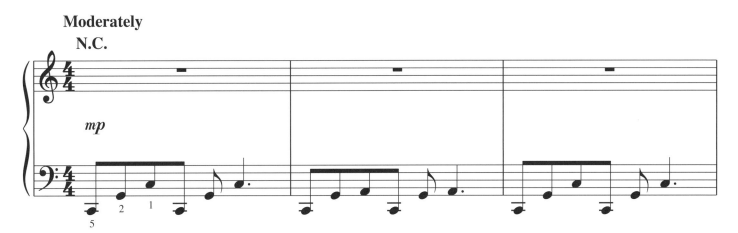

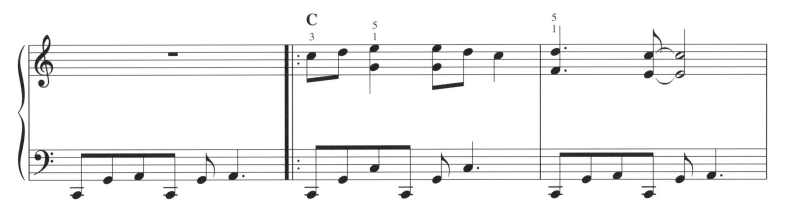

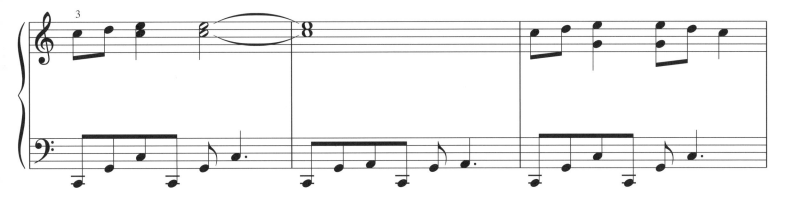

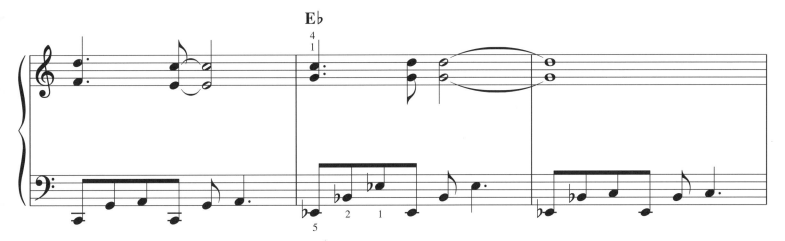

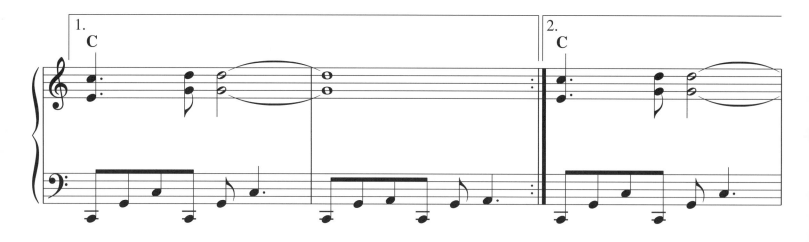

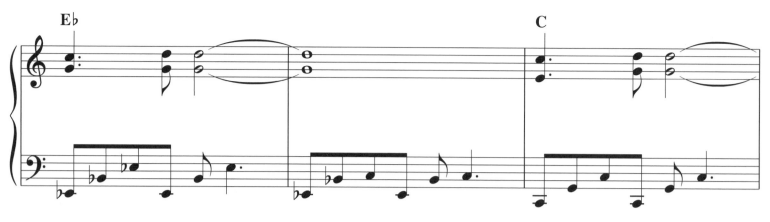

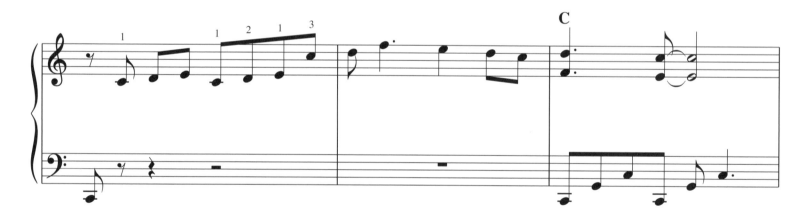

CHRISTMAS TIME IS HERE

Words by LEE MENDELSON
Music by VINCE GUARALDI

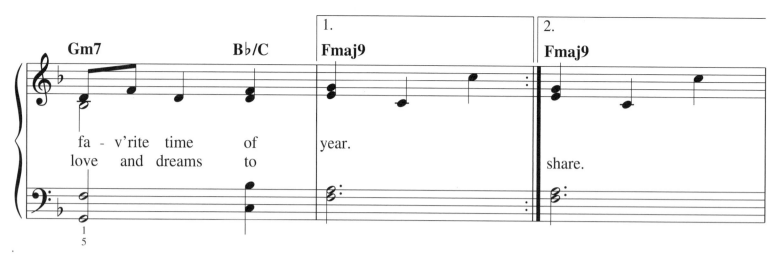

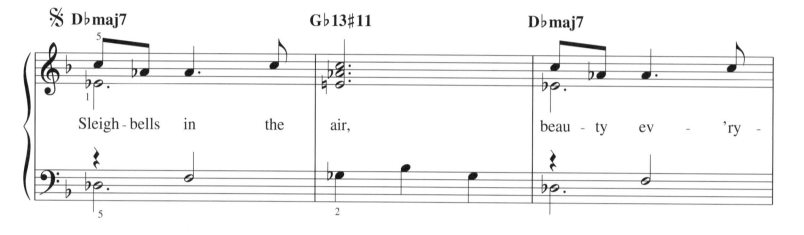

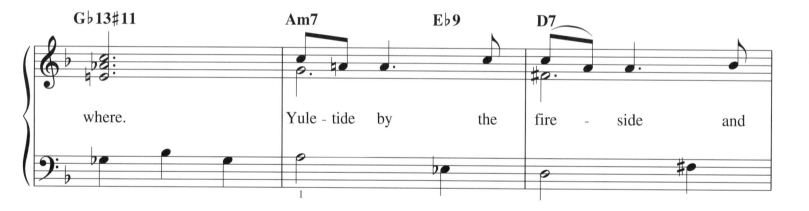

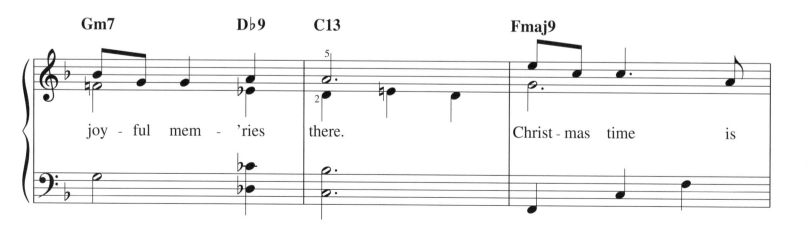

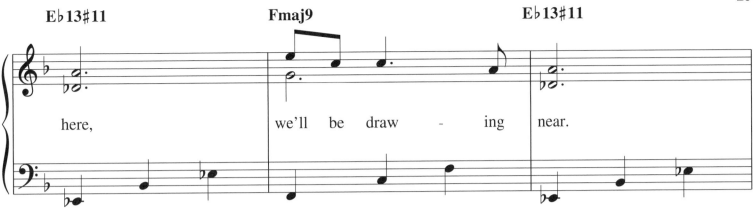

here, we'll be draw - ing near.

To Coda ⊕

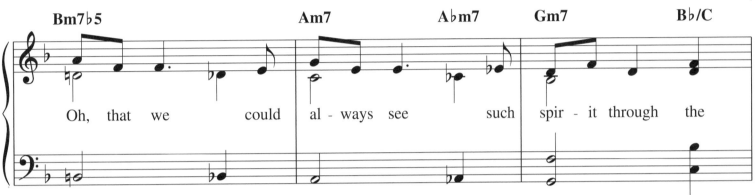

Oh, that we could al - ways see such spir - it through the

year. *(Instrumental)*

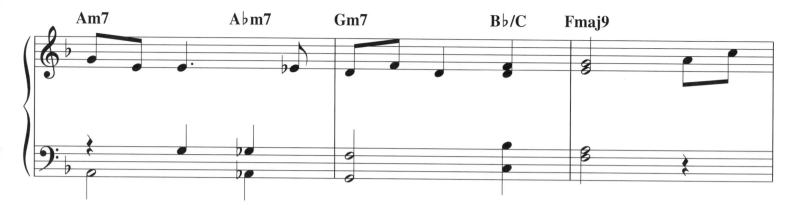

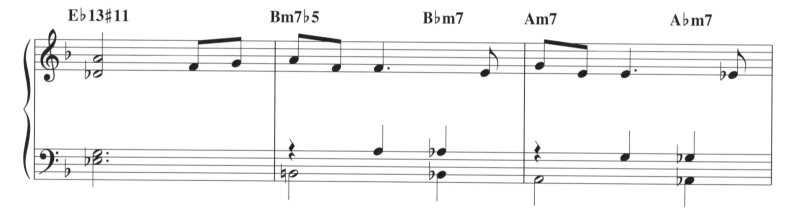

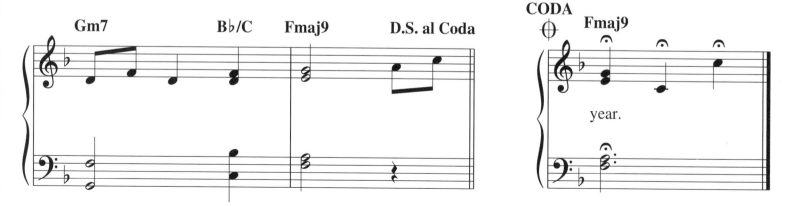

SKATING

By VINCE GUARALDI

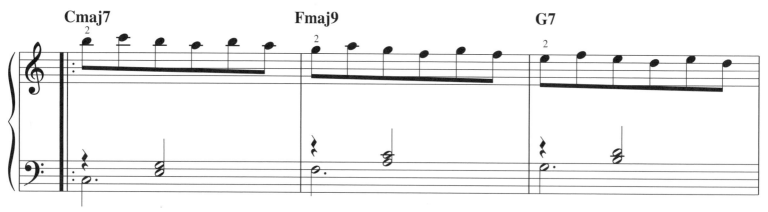

With pedal

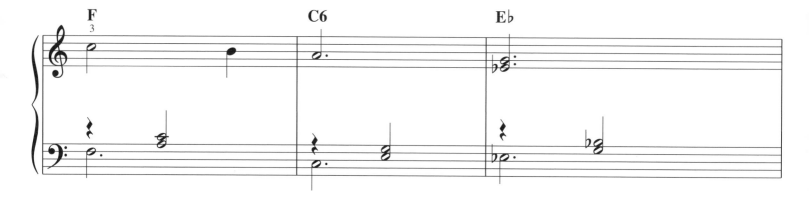

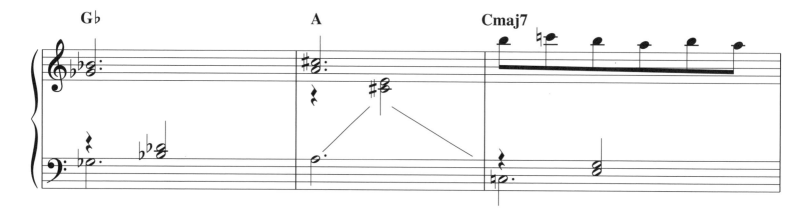

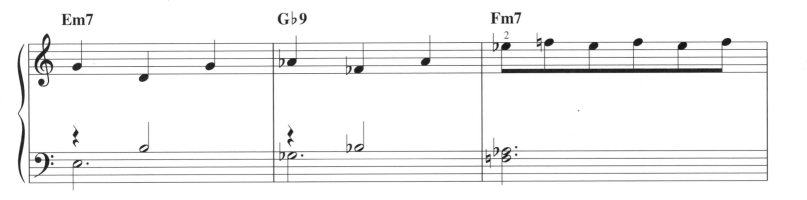

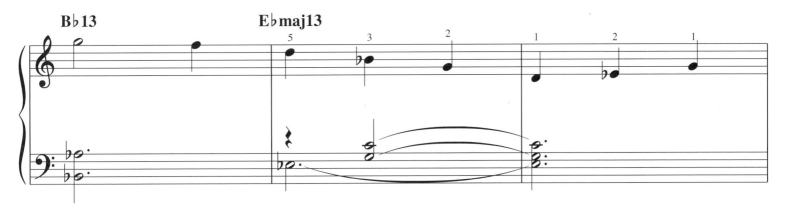

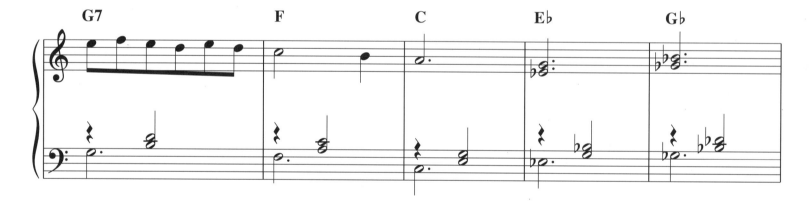

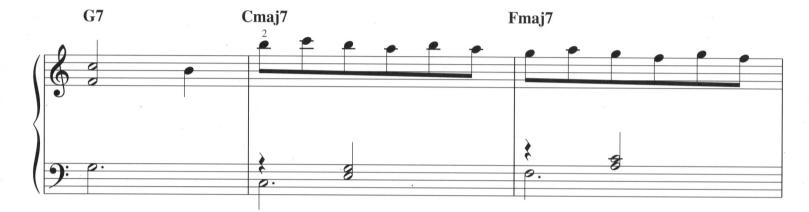

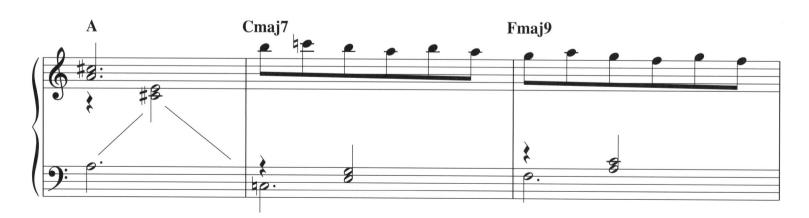

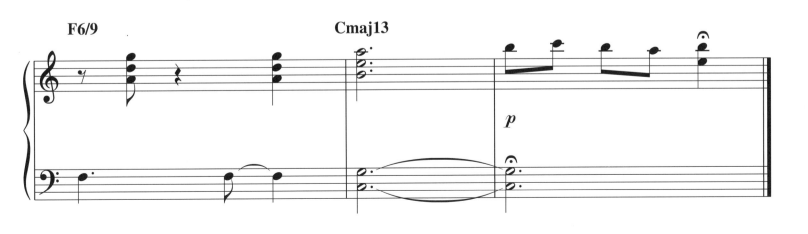

HARK, THE HERALD ANGELS SING

Traditional
Arranged by VINCE GUARALDI

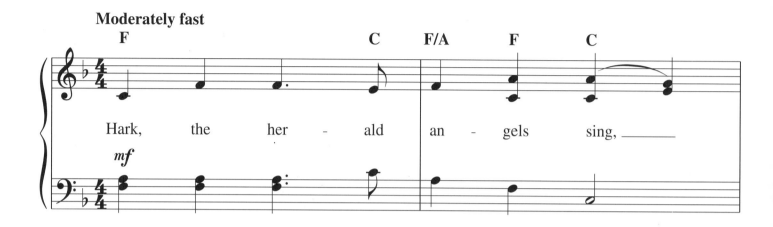

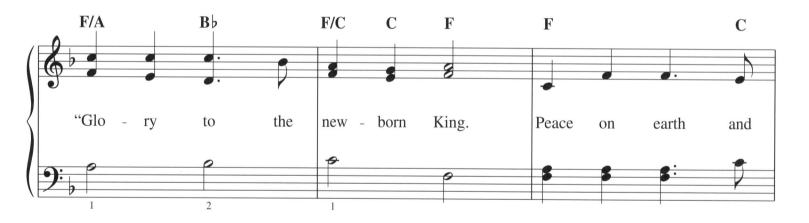

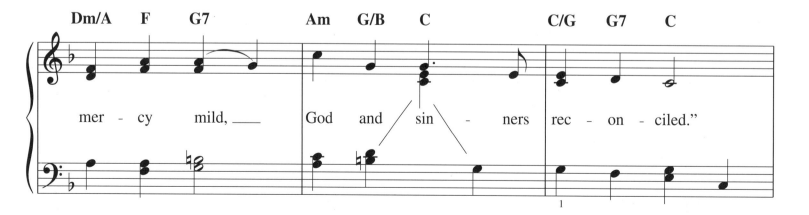

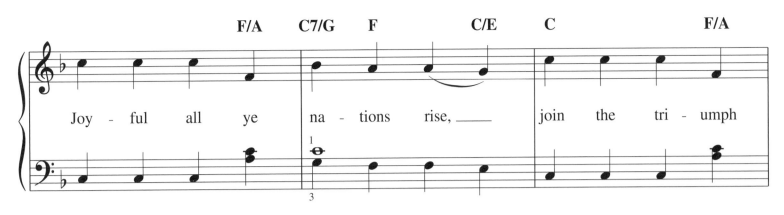

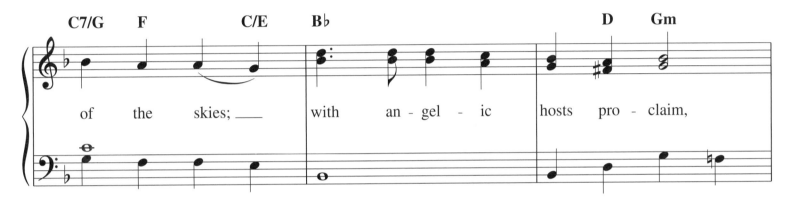

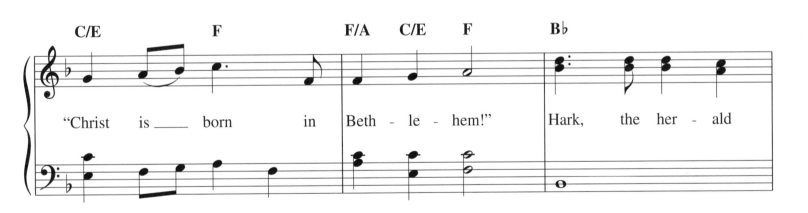

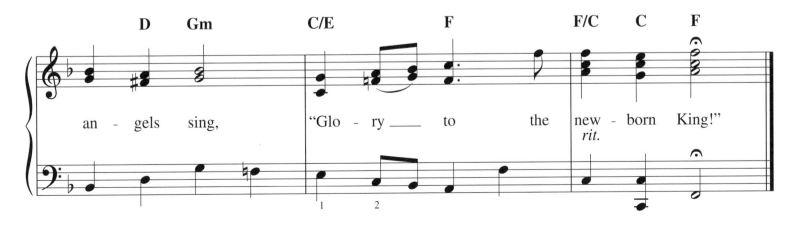

FÜR ELISE

By BEETHOVEN
Arranged by VINCE GUARALDI

THE CHRISTMAS SONG
(Chestnuts Roasting on an Open Fire)

Music and Lyric by MEL TORME
and ROBERT WELLS

With much expression

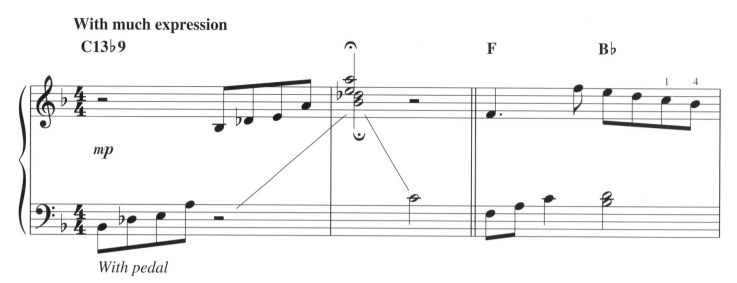

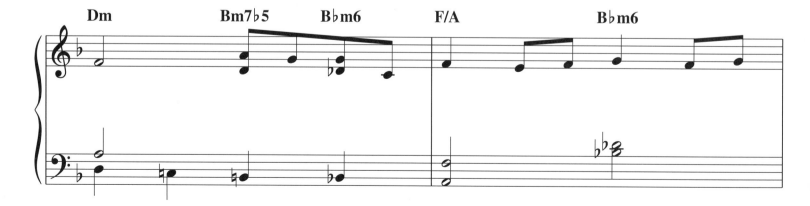

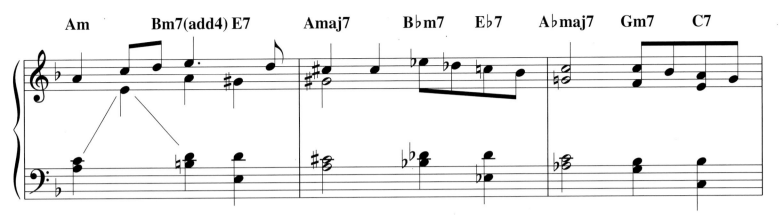

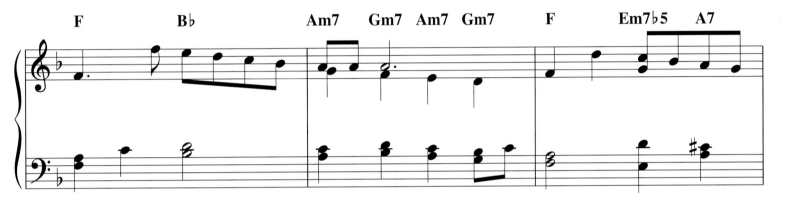

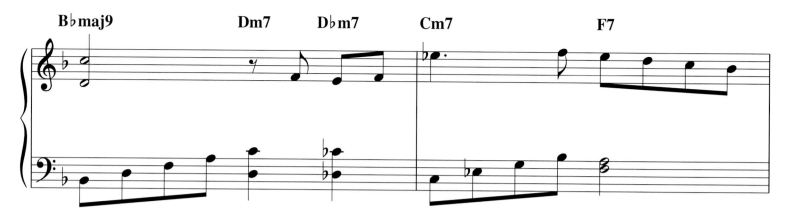

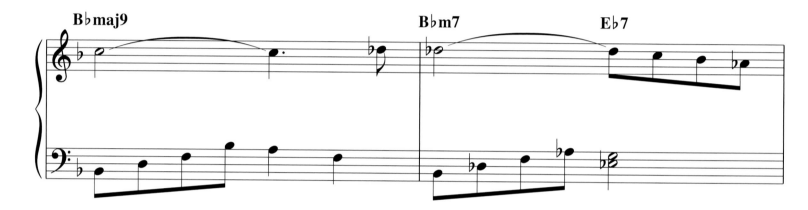

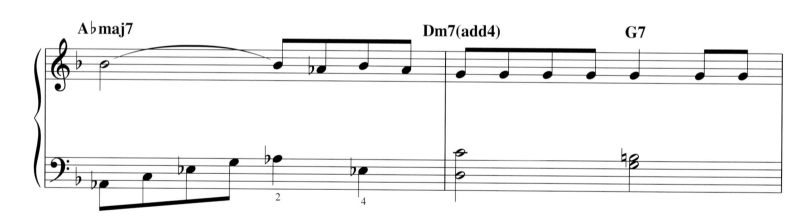

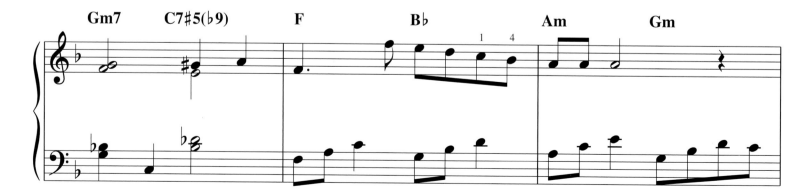

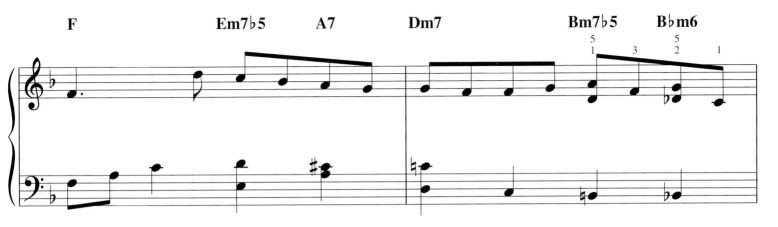

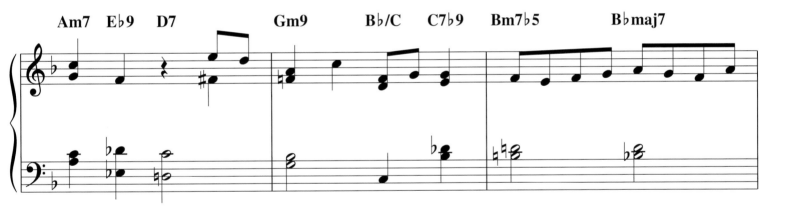

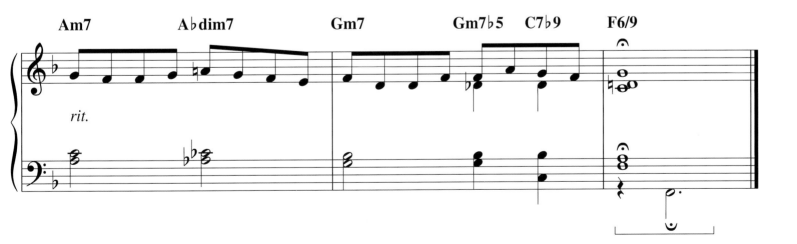

CHRISTMAS IS COMING

By VINCE GUARALDI

Bright Bossa

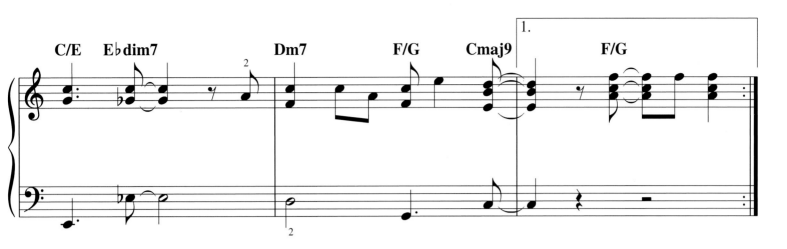

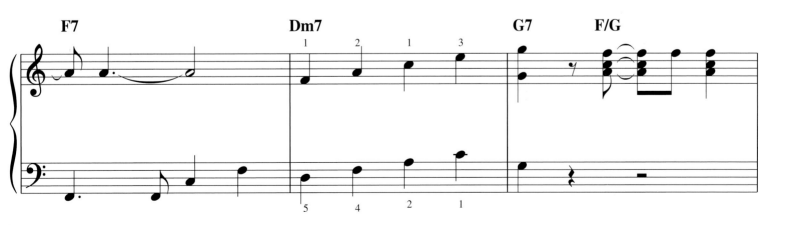

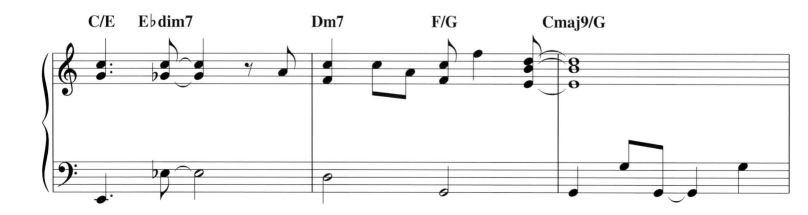

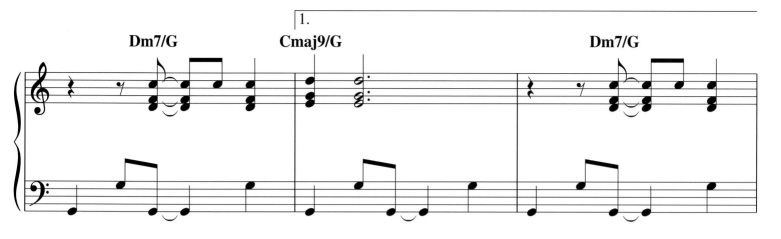

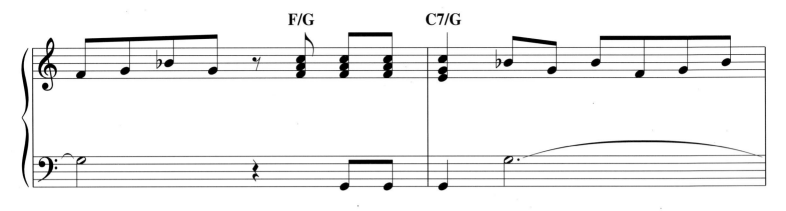

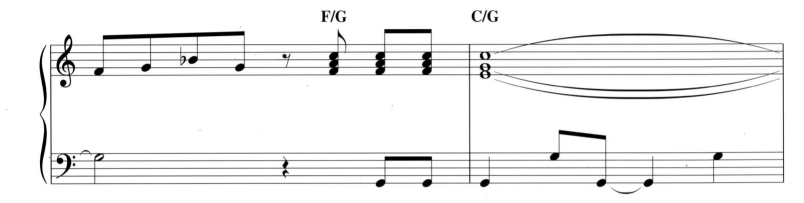

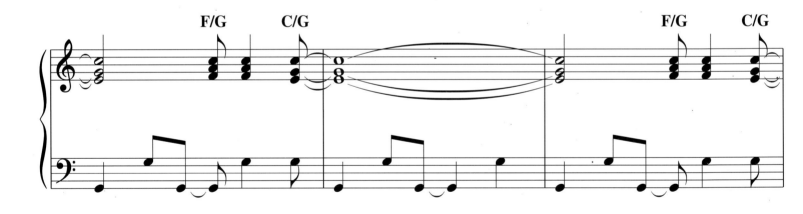